The Glassblower's House

Matt Bryden

Matt Bryden lives in Devon. He has published a
pamphlet *Night Porter* (Templar), a first collection *Boxing the
Compass* (Templar) and a book of translations *The Desire to Sing
after Sunset* (ShowWe).

First Published in 2023
By Live Canon Poetry Ltd
www.livecanon.co.uk

978-1-909703-22-3

A CIP catalogue record for this book is available from the British Library.

Contents

Early Days

Today I heard my son's heartbeat.
A piston. Pure, its own pace.

Or my daughter's heartbeat.
She bounces on her back like a girl;

but I feel it is my son.
Already, he can swallow, hiccup, hear —

has been snuck along the Quantocks,
swept in a purse along Bicknoller Combe.

His mother carries an exhaustion she denies,
inhabits its centre, is brought up sharp.

Sat off track, she eats the donut she's saved,
magnificent in her self-control.

Battles each evening, her ears sore; snuffles
through a strengthened immune system.

Sleeps longer, more.

Janus

Cheap wine and dangling my feet in the swimming pool,
    urination and tilting the glass for another pull,
clean pair of heels reading *don't worry, I'll call.*

The white lakes are clear.
    And this, the sea of seven colours.
The orbital range of the Charioteer.

Since when did two heads sit on one neck,
    finger and thumb break a psalter's back?
Take this –

the eye with an eye in the back of the head,
    the knuckle's pink hinge at the incubator's lid,
the glass sides of what I did.

Crossing the Owl's Bridge

So I took the circular path –
wary, as Mabel sniffed the grass,
that this was the time for badgers.

And she knew something extraordinary
had happened, keeping close to me –
the hushed lanes and closed rock roses.

'Keep the owl from the birthing room,'
the *Day by Day* pregnancy guide told us,
grown fancy with folklore, brimful

with vernix, lashes and harbingers of doom.
'Don't forget,' its Focus on Men instructed,
'it's not all about you.'

As I left theatre, a nurse slotted
my mobile back in my palm.
I re-traced the scene:

how the poorly administered cannula
hurt more than the lumbar puncture.
How there was always a risk of bleeding.

How the green plastic sheet spread,
separating upper and lower halves,
non-absorbent, occluding the view –

stripped of horizon, the light source invisible
on our still serviceable path,
the fields glowing and burnished.

Finally, we came to the straight
where the alley goes deep, becomes a holloway overcast
with trees, warrens built into banks of clay.

Your pitch of voles and baby rabbits.

Owl heard among houses to herald the fall of unmarried maidens;
hibou grand duc with full epaulettes, down covering feet and legs
right to the leading edge of the wing;

       you dispatch almost in silence

incubate your clutch alone;
dive bomb us now, secure your tunnel, bloody our milk.
We are sorry to set foot on your patch.

         For now our vulnerable bellies are exposed.

Sometimes I play with your reach –
hold a fingertip to a flame, my face to the water,
slip one leg then another over the ticker-taped *Keep Out.*

And do I detect you (who can live to sixteen
but rarely make two) also wear a band carved
against your innermost talon, contracting you

even as it marks you out for death,

       you who call to give us fair warning,
            who try to keep us clear?

Four Weeks

Her company as I silently defeat the computer at chess.

*

With the exhaustion, how can I savour her warm smell,
her single milk mind?
I crowd her with the sound of water, birdsong.

*

To sit her at a site makes a story of anything –
a sailor by the river awaiting her coracle;
a singer backstage post-show;
a dipsomaniac after feeding,
twenty-pints-to-the-good and worse for wear.

*

Manically, the mother runs through her chores:
bathing, changing, feeding, yet avoids the one thing
that might relieve her for a couple of hours, expressing.
Pictures of a woman scrubbing and scrubbing her hands
at a tap before crumpling in tears.

*

I take her for a walk in a loose-fitting tangerine hat.
The sun would bake her unprotected brain.
We move fast, under the eye, along the river's mazy course.
An egret, fastidious in its slowness, sidesteps
out of the river, fine white against green.

*

The mother is crowded with kisses –
strains through the windscreen,
a press of cars behind. Waking,
she sits herself upright,
contemplates my sleeping face
and pokes me in the eye.

Vertigo

In the nineteen-twenties and -fifties
a prevalence of private detectives.

She threw herself into the San Francisco Bay
in a fit of admiration.

A white steering wheel beneath the hands,
the Golden Gate Bridge projected

against a technicolour wash.
You could be forgiven for losing

your balance. Alone in the house,
clothes becoming old and dirty

it is hard to break upon her trance.
What was there inside that told you to jump?

The dissolve into her white coat.
Application of lavender gloves.

The PI swims to find out how she slipped
his trail, and finding himself

before the backboard of a painting,
rounds upon her and a part of himself:

You shouldn't have been so sentimental.

Portugal

It's not the way a river tends to downhill
has us walking at tilt,
that snow as pure as one to one part in ten
slips from the slatted clouds

so much as her belonging
to another climate and fruit;

and when the doctor folded back
his sleeves, the bloodless skin
pinned against the dressing, a pale star
about a gaping hole,

the gulf in her abdomen
was the exact shape of a horse
kicking at stable. Reaching in, he lifted it
clean of the signalling sides

where it coiled, moulded
like a mollusc of white chocolate,

and at arm's length
rotated it across the room,
set it down in the straw.

Rabbits

A strangely contentless Chinese New Year.
We walked through the thronged streets
past a woman cleaning both sides of a glass door.
A close-haired man clutched a water and ice.
I eyed the art students outside Soho,
hems running clavicle to navel –
considered paying a prostitute, asking
her to go slower, be less professional.

As a child-like dancer fell backwards
and the chatter mounted, I told you
I needed to feel you commit to me.
A star chart held a zodiac of fortunes:
Rabbits, it said, *this will be a hard astrology.*

The Glassblower's House

In the glassblower's house
where the ten-year-old pushed a little girl
who fell from the wall and died,
the mother became an alcoholic;
and now he drinks carrot champagne
with his wife in the freezing kitchen,
cold coming in from the garden,
an arbour completely contained.

His father made jewellery
and sold glass bricks
to drop into swimming pools
and measure how the water rose.
Only children, with their acuity of sight,
would be hired to demonstrate
the principle of displaced density,
the ties binding sports, maths and physics.

My lurcher off its lead
burst a hedgerow and down the steep banks
managed to tie herself in wire,
the evening quiet but for her panting
as she lay on her side;
and I glimpsed inside the globe:
the pristine pond, the rising steps
leading to the glassblower's house.

Where there were still shields
from the science department
mounted on wood,
frozen photographs
of extended family,
and there amidst them, the girl
before the gravel was removed from the drive
and replaced with a more dependable surface.

And the wife is an immaculate cook –
smell her shaved parmesan –
view them sat on high stools
before drums of Illy espresso,
the lawn after dark,
after the champagne,
a stretch of beach visited by curlews,
rocks that remind you of the Highlands.

And in the innermost room
in consummation
three children are produced
under the pressure of diamonds;
they tear through the rooms
as if through a museum,
no attention paid to
the glass cabinets, the high vases.

I recall a grandmother
watching television
as children took sweets
from the shelf above her head
then ran behind the door to eat them;
soon were jumping over her,
stepping between her thighs;
and she didn't move at all,

didn't react, say anything
as they plundered the cubes of fudge.
After several hours, when they heard
their own mother in the hall
ask, 'How were they?'
the three children were quite taken aback
as she spat out, 'They were dreadful! Just dreadful!'
and burst into tears.

But that memory is behind a curtain.
The glassblower's house
has gardens with canes,
celery, cress, larders with yellow curd in jars,
sacks of flour and nuts,
tinfoil pierced by beaks.
And those who visit might see
children with glinting wings waving wands –

with one stroke of which they might
disappear and teleport
to another room in the house –
like itinerant sheep in the facing fields.
As croquet hoops sink through soil
and running shoes puncture the sod,
we are all nurses in the purlieu
of the glassblower's house.

Thin smoke – almost horizontal –
from the chimney, over a granary of gems.
The lawn pressed between leaves.
As frozen sheets make to billow
and pondweed rots,
no stone may shatter the glazing
nor release the tongue
from its gate latch entrance, its simple key.

Centres of Gravity

I try to lift my head from her crib,
its skewed soft toys hung from a rail,
and transfer my thoughts elsewhere.

My eyes and neck won't let me.
No dispensation has me break my watch.
Holding her close to feel her breath

I cannot see her, though she seizes
the arm of my glasses with articulacy, arrests
the drop of a bib by its green silk ribbon

in a fist she releases only
with difficulty; a feat of instinct –
like Mabel covering the fields as a puppy.

You, in the Altogether
(iterations of a future daughter)

Amelia Earhart through mist
I saw you slip past me
in the direction of the restrooms.

These days, I offer up your image on my phone
like a cup or talisman;
the face of my child stands for something.

You've been a while.
And is that a hand-drier
or a coffee machine's laboured breath

as you pull and pull at that blue towel
swallowed and re-swallowed
to leave another untouched strip?

You have a Spanish face, it squeezes
into expressions of kindness.
I see you side-saddle at a petrol pump,

your boyfriend gone to the kiosk to pay;
or on a Triumph, its brown tank rising
between your legs as you smile and rev.

There is distance between here and the glass.
I'm aware of an upstairs, though no feet
pass over me.

As others use their voices without trying
and the level grain of the table
supports my writing arm, I look up

to the light which runs the room towards me,
catches my retinas, my ring,
and I register the young.

You are a long time coming.

*

My storied maid,
you on your high legs
waiting at the counter.

I tot you up from where
your calves cross the daylight –
taut wire, high grasses –

to your capital brain
as it tallies syrups and ices.
You who are leaving the way you came.

In southern Chile, a season of rain
keeps you to the house;
you cannot see the mountain peaks

and your big-boned baby
suffers pressure
alongside the plaster.

By dropping a pin point upon you
or kicking a wedge of sand
from your door

I do you a disservice.
You are the girl whose damson blood
runs the teeth of her comb.

Though equally you nurse a cup
amidst your two forked friends
who turn and, in silhouette,

cast themselves deep into the room.

*

There was just the faintest creak
when I honed in on you,
hushed in a transit van

on a Devonshire lane
as the trail of a meteor pulsed once
against the felt then fell back and faded...

but I had been reading a book of proverbs
claiming one has to wish instantaneously
(and that shooting stars meant ill)

so I packed away and lobbed myself
onto your back seat
like a lunchbox bound with a canvas strap,

the lanes under starlight their own silver pond,
the cherry stem tying
road ahead to road behind.

Ankles crossed, my daughter
lies in her crib,
one bandaged hand behind her head.

At the wood's edge, the owls
in her mind meet the one
whose call we pause for

that she has yet to see.

A Preservation Spell

Should sandal pass the chalk outline,
the lamp's limit – should a ribbon's fall
draw your passage from the world

then it is all like snow – the lie
no indicator of depth where it settles,
laughter tumbling as the body tips face-down;

and our calculations come in hunches,
the strike of the quarter-jacks crossing the river
in imminence of rain; the devil sat in his hammock

just beneath the nail. Remember the animals
in our windows at the knees of the saints,
how they reflect each one's pomposity and grace –

the goose at the end of a golden cord, the man himself
set for a parade to demonstrate his quiddity.
We secured your knowledge to follow men like them.

So pride does not come into it – if you prosper
it has little to do with our handiwork,
regardless how we sank canes into the soil,

ran channels, led you by your open hand.
Our superstitions the stuff of donkeys
hung from trees, cotton sewn through lips

and mountain lions; in defiance of which
we tease out your locks like seedlings,
dress you in linens tailored in a feminine style.

The Screen

Say my wife and daughter went before me.
The little one sat in the arms of her mother.
But the turnstiles and slipping of shoes
I could not watch. An ice bath of tin.
Could not get into my child's eyes,
however wide, stooped level with her.
She is all about observing.
I'd drive back, the wipers full tilt,
sat nav taking me via Dancing Lane,
soul sat high up in my sternum
peeping out my throat. I'd sing and sing
make the glasses in the kitchen ring with it.
She will take her first steps in Chãos,
amid stray dogs and tinkling children.
And me the other side of a screen.

Taster

During the pregnancy, my wife's palate
was clean as the white goods section of Dixons.

Stood inside a cubicle of light, a room
in the Tate Modern, we watched

walls shift colour: red to blue, pink to green.
Felt the tip and tilt of ground moving under us.

Then a smaller white cubicle cleansed
the palate of our eyes so, on exiting,

we didn't stumble into traffic.
Now our baby sleeps in a coracle of light,

her crib draped with Corleone lace.
Our ginger female transports fleas to it, urinates in it,

leaves shrews in the antechamber.
We strip, rinse and spray.

This chilli has a good kick, my wife tells me,
we should serve it for your family unawares.

Jam our tender taste buds to the limit.
Funnel the brown powder into the pan.

Hats

In the Portuguese stables, a snowflake design – a working hat.
You'd wake at 5 am, drink a steaming tea
and work till evening when you ate
a soup of vegetables which tasted of sun.

I've lost too many dogs, you'd tell me.
Poisoned or beaten to death,
trapped the other side of a metal door,
shelved in the hold of a plane.

Porlock Weir. A pebble shore.
Catfish choking on the beach.
I see the breadth of your cutting loose:
head tilted towards a pillbox, your voice trying it out.

And have lost my own.
Wouldn't you want to be there with your daughter, yes,
and me? Photos show the brilliant light,
unsparing space: room for no shortage of others.

We came here together more than once.
Without a thumb-stick, you tired quickly.
I offered the crook of an arm. Our dog already erased
at the edges. I imagined, still in the city,

how the best prize of all would be
a key, access to every museum and café –
But don't you see, you say, the sofa and settee glaring
that early January day, *I don't want to do those things with you?*

Reading *The Secret Garden* to Amelia

Colin, your restoration's unease –
still that smell of mothballs on you,
the censer-dust of Lourdes. How long
into your recovery till you roll up your sleeves?

These picture books, four frames to a row
four rows to a page, are like Braille.
A certain progress is made
before the index finger returns to its place.

And in the retelling, Mary's tears will come
at the same stage. Her stubbornness
impregnates my daughter – *Yes, you will
hear it!* – in just the same way

as wet-haired and night-dressed
after her bath, I tell her,
'I want to see you readying for rest
and settling down, not jumping

on the bed,' and the lesson sinks in
(now Colin can walk, his father's love
is restored) and head against pillow
she adopts Mary's words: *It wasn't wanted.*

Keynote

A girl, dropped from space with her own smile,
can hear a recording by Aretha
and from the riffle of applause

distinguish a single hand-clap,
the root note of the chord,
put her hands together and proceed

to give her tribute across the universe,
stepping lightly with her old soft shoe.
That girl possesses

a facility of mind – an inner sight –
to pick out the Evening Star
unflummoxed by astral chatter,

to cast a line through the pack ice's one hole.
From the swarm of crickets, castanets
and swirl of pistachio scoop

identify the fall of a single domino tile.
Aspires to the nuclear family
even as locks are changed and uprooted

stumps of horseradish rot in the grass;
a key-ring –
tossed like a mobile phone

in pique – sinks through the nettle grasp
by the raised beds, the border fence
encircling a forty-hectare view.

Epicentre

One of your best traits: a readiness for cheering.

In *Little Women*, for example, as the extempore
'Ding Dong Merrily on High' trails off,
a carriageway thinning to a single lane,

you are there to applaud, catching
the flame like an Olympic torch
(it's a long film, and Beth is not even dead yet…)

In musical movement, you give your all.
Your single-minded dance is intended,
strangely Sumo. After you handed Mabel

the lamb hearts in her bowl, entire,
we stood agape, juice spurting
from the purple muscle, the dog's jaws working

to gain purchase and saw. Felt
exuberant, not considering the after-ripple
which would surely come. That evening,

when her whimpering climbed the stairs,
you were past all care.
And later, as Somerset was rocked by a 4.3,

your mother and I could hear
the plates ten miles down, the epicentre
over in Bridgwater;

and she stood in silence, strangely moved
at the Juliet balcony. I was excluded,
like when we arrived at the new house

and she could not, would not, hear me.
The following morning, the radio
informed us of what had been

and we lowered the piano lid
having run our hands along the keys.

A Clean Break

This is how it's done. Invite her to a park
but first enjoy a tour of the Greek Golden Age.
When she arrives she'll have a bike
making greeting awkward –
notice later, it's a Raleigh *Amazon*
(think Penthesilea). It's a good bike.
Don't mention Anne of Cleves.
Bounce off her enthusiasm. She will be guarded,

yet dance about it on a ticking clock.
Until she asks who will look after your cat
(time is getting away) it's all politesse
and how much thought has she given it,
she who once let herself into a friend's house
unheralded, and scared her half to death.

She said we'd meet again
and I'm letting her score this point;
and if we really are both having the last look,
then know she is the one getting away.
Our park is hidden, close by
her London college. We used to play cards,
could be spotted in a little hideaway.
Hers was a *Thatchers*; we'd pore over crosswords.

She will look immediate arriving on her bike –
there is no not knowing it is her;
she from whom time is getting away
will glitter and depart. We remember
so much about each other, but are denied the evening.
Drinking makes her sad, brimming to conclusion
as now, riding the cusp of herself

knowing that if I were single.
Our thoughts turned to visas, salad days and estaminets.
The King was wily enough to inveigle
his wife, of Cleves, to divorce him
and it is said at later meetings
they pursued games of cards.
I am not sure who brought the deck.

Blind Spot

'He took the preliminary precaution of having his wife
watched by a private detective.' *Vertigo*

So he shadows a quarry, her eyes on the prize,
parks at a discreet five metres,
palms his Homburg at the entrance,
the graveyard otherwise empty –
pulls away after waiting for the ignition to fire.

Though each injured soul thinks it theirs alone
to diagnose another's injury,
it is as she seems to slip her bonds
she slips into her role more deeply.

Notes

'Janus' – the two-headed God (who gives us the name 'January') looks both back at the year that has passed and forwards to the year to come.

'Crossing the Owl's Bridge' – a native American idiom for death. A column in the *Day-by-Day Pregnancy Book* (Dorling Kindersley) advises prospective parents to keep owls from the birthing room for fear of ill-omen.

'*Vertigo*' – quotations are taken from the Alfred Hitchcock film.

'Rabbits' – counterintuitively, the Chinese Year of the Rabbit does not necessarily promise to be a good one for Rabbits.

'Taster' – the exhibition referenced is by Olafur Eliasson.

'The Screen' – Chãos is a village in Santarém, Portugal.

Acknowledgements

Thanks to Martha Sprackland for editing an early version of this manuscript; to Pascale Petit, whose workshop led to the writing of 'Crossing the Owl's Bridge;' to Cahal Dallat and students on the Between the Lines course, whose comments informed several of these poems; to Carrie Etter for editing a later version of this manuscript; to Dixie Darch for her friendship and for giving me a roof over my head to write some of these poems; to Taunton's Fire River Poets for their kindness and support, in particular John Stuart and Graeme Ryan; to Mike Duggan, Sophie Nicholls and Anke Laufer; and to fellow Tertulians Harry Man, Nikita Lalwani and Ros Wynne-Jones.

'*Vertigo*' and 'Early Days' first appeared in *Finished Creatures*; 'Janus' was published in the *London Reader*; 'Crossing the Owl's Bridge' won the Charroux Memoir Prize 2020; 'Four Weeks' appeared in Issue One of *The Crank*; 'A Preservation Spell' was commended in the Café Writers Competition 2019; 'Rabbits' appeared in *Goldfish*; 'Centres of Gravity' and 'Blind Spot' appeared in *Seisma*; 'Keynote' appeared (as 'Keynot') in Voyage 4 of Glyn Maxwell's *Dark Canadee*, available at the Poetry School website.